September 11, 2001

CORNERSTONES
OF FREEDOM

SECOND SERIES

Andrew Santella

Children's Press
An Imprint of Scholastic Inc.
New York • Toronto • London • Auckland • Sydney
Mexico City • New Delhi • Hong Kong
Danbury, Connecticut

Photographs © 2002: AP/Wide World Photos: 18 bottom (APTV), 12 (J. Pat Carter), 37 (Lionel Cironneau), 6 top (Gino Domenico), 23 (Ron Frehm), 30, 19 top left (Danny Johnston), 39 (Beth A. Keiser), 32 (Kenneth Lambert), cover bottom, cover top (Mark Lennihan), 41 (Catherine Leuthild), 26 bottom center (Joe Marquette), 3, 7, 14, 45 bottom (Doug Mills), 20 top right; Corbis Images: 18 top, 26 bottom right, 34 bottom (AFP), 26 top (Paul Almasy), 27 top right (Kelly Harriger), 28 (Robert Holmes), 25 (Angelo Hornak), 24 (James Marshall), 11, 15, 18 center, 19 bottom, 20 bottom, 20 top left, 21, 22, 26 bottom left, 29, 34 top, 44 right, 44 left (Reuters NewMedia Inc.), 6 bottom (Bill Ross), 4 right (Lee Snider), 27 bottom (Paul A. Souders), 4 left (Mark Thiessen), 19 top right (David & Peter Turnley), 5; Stone/Getty Images/Joseph Pobereskin: 10, 45 top right; The Image Works: 8, 45 left (Rob Crandall), 36.

Library of Congress Cataloging-in-Publication Data

Santella, Andrew.

September 11, 2001 / Andrew Santella.

p. cm. — (Cornerstones of freedom. Second series)

Summary: Recounts events of September 11, 2001, when terrorists flew into the World Trade Center and the Pentagon, discusses what is known of the terrorists, and relates how America has responded to the tragedy. Includes bibliographical references and index.

ISBN-13: 978-0-516-22692-7 (lib. bdg.)   978-0-531-18692-3 (pbk.)

ISBN-10: 0-516-22692-4 (lib. bdg.)   0-531-18692-X (pbk.)

1. September 11 Terrorist Attacks, 2001—Juvenile literature. 2.Terrorism—United States—Juvenile literature. [1. September 11 Terrorist Attacks, 2001. 2. Terrorism.] I. Title. II. Series.

HV6432 .S26 2002

973.931—dc21

2002004742

14 15 16 17 18 R 19 18 17 16

THE EVENTS OF SEPTEMBER 11, 2001, shocked and horrified Americans. They served as a reminder that even a nation as mighty as the United States must always be prepared to defend itself. President Bush spoke for the nation when he said, "None of us will ever forget this day."

The White House and the U.S. Capitol, two symbols of American democracy located in Washington, D.C.

Tuesday, September 11, 2001, began like any ordinary day in the United States. In Washington, D.C., tourists lined up outside the White House and the Capitol. They waited to visit the buildings that symbolize American democracy for people all around the world.

Across the river in Arlington, Virginia, the workday began at the Pentagon, the massive five-sided building that is the headquarters of the United States Department of

Defense. The nation's top military officials work there, keeping the United States safe. Early in the morning of September 11, they were already at work in their offices.

In New York City the banks and business offices of Wall Street buzzed with activity. The southern tip of Manhattan Island in New York City is the business center of America, its skyscrapers are concrete symbols of the wealth of the

The Pentagon, the headquarters of the U.S. Department of Defense, was one of the buildings attacked on September 11.

Wall Street, the heart of New York City's financial district

United States. On September 11 no buildings in New York City stood taller than the twin towers of the World Trade Center. Each tower of the World Trade Center stretched 110 stories high. That morning, more than forty thousand workers, about as many people as live in a small city, made their way up the elevators of the giant buildings.

In Sarasota, Florida, President George W. Bush was beginning his workday, too. He had traveled from Washington to

The view of Manhattan across the East River at night. Notice the twin towers on the right, standing taller than all the other buildings.

President Bush's Chief of Staff Andrew Card whispers into his ear to give him the news of the crashes at the World Trade Center.

Florida to visit Emma E. Booker Elementary School. He was there to talk to students about the importance of education.

Airports all over the country were busy that morning, as well. Travelers waited to board airplanes that would carry them to business meetings or vacation destinations or to visit loved ones.

A large portion of the Pentagon was ripped away by the crash.

DAY OF TERROR

September 11, 2001, was one of the most tragic and awful days in American history. That morning terrorists attacked the World Trade Center in New York City and the Pentagon outside Washington. Their weapons were airplanes filled with innocent passengers and loaded with **explosive** jet fuel. Four teams of terrorists **hijacked** four airplanes that day. One by one, the terrorists turned the planes into flying bombs. Their targets were symbols of American power and wealth. The terrorists crashed one plane into the north tower and another into the south tower of the World Trade Center.

8

They flew another plane into the side of the Pentagon. A fourth hijacked plane was probably headed for one of the important government buildings in Washington, D.C. However, the plane crashed in a field in western Pennsylvania before it could reach its target. Passengers on board the plane fought the hijackers to keep them from attacking Washington.

The attacks brought the towers of the World Trade Center crashing down. The plane ripped a huge hole in one side of the Pentagon, setting the building on fire. All the passengers and all the terrorists on each plane were killed, as were thousands of people in and around the World Trade Center. More than one hundred others lost their lives in the Pentagon. The destruction was so great at the World Trade Center that it was difficult to get an accurate count of the dead. After the attacks, officials estimated that 2,983 people had died.

ASSAULT ON THE WORLD TRADE CENTER

Just before eight o'clock on the morning of September 11, an American Airlines plane took off from Logan Airport in Boston. It was Flight 11, making its daily trip across the country to Los Angeles. (Airlines assign numbers to their flights.) To cover the 3,000 miles (4,828 kilometers) between Boston and Los Angeles, the plane carried thousands of gallons of fuel. There were eleven crew members and eighty-one passengers on board

THE WORLD TRADE CENTER

The World Trade Center was a complex of seven buildings in New York City. The two biggest and most famous buildings in the complex were a pair of 110-story towers, which came to be called the twin towers. The north tower was completed in 1972. The south tower was completed in 1973. They were home to dozens of law firms, banks, insurance companies, and other businesses. In fact, the World Trade Center was one of the largest business centers in the world. The towers were so large that each had more than 100 elevators.

The twin towers as they stood before the attacks

* * * *

Flight 11. Later the world learned that five of those passengers were terrorists determined to kill themselves and thousands of innocent people.

Flight 11 never made it to Los Angeles. No one knows for sure what happened on Flight 11, but this much is known: A few minutes into the flight the plane changed direction. Instead of continuing west to Los Angeles, the plane turned south. It was now pointed straight at New York City. The five terrorists, perhaps armed with knives, had taken control of the plane, and one of them was flying it. The plane was moving so fast that in just a few minutes Flight 11 was over New York. Later, witnesses reported seeing a plane flying very fast and very low toward lower Manhattan. At 8:45 A.M. Flight 11 crashed into the north tower of the World Trade Center. The plane's impact ripped a huge hole in the face of the tower, and the fuel on board the plane **ignited**. It exploded in a huge fireball. Flame and smoke poured from the building. Inside the burning building, thousands of workers tried to escape down elevators and staircases. Many never made it, trapped by fire, smoke, and intense heat.

On the streets below, thousands of people looked on in horror as the building burned. Some had seen the plane hit the building. Most people thought that the crash must have been an accident.

Residents of Oklahoma City watch the coverage of September 11 as they wait to donate blood to the victims of the attack.

* * * *

However, at 9:03 A.M., it became clear that this was not an accident. At that moment a second plane crashed, this one into the south tower. It was United Airlines Flight 175. It too had taken off from Logan Airport in Boston just before eight o'clock. It too had been headed for Los Angeles loaded with jet fuel. It too had been hijacked by terrorists.

By the time Flight 175 crashed, thousands of **onlookers** had gathered on the streets of Manhattan. Fire trucks and ambulances had arrived to rescue victims of the crash. Millions were watching the scene on television in their homes. They saw the plane tear through the wall of the tower and disappear inside. They saw another huge ball of fire erupt. A shower of metal and concrete fell from the building. By now it was clear that the United States was under attack.

THE PRESIDENT REACTS

At the same time, President George W. Bush was meeting the second-graders of Booker Elementary School in Sarasota, Florida. He was listening to the class read aloud when Flight 175 crashed in New York. Minutes later, one of his aides whispered the news in the president's ear.

Slowly the rest of the nation was learning the horrible news, too. Bush made a statement in front of television news cameras, hoping to reassure the people of the United States. "This is a difficult time for America," the president said. He promised that the government would "hunt down the folks who committed this act."

Air Force One, the
president's plane

First, the president's protectors had to see to his safety. No one knew if the president himself might be a target of the terrorists. His Secret Service guards took extra precautions. They searched the president's plane, Air Force One, for bombs. The president planned to return to Washington to direct the government's response to the crisis. But before he could return, the nation's capital came under attack.

ATTACK ON THE PENTAGON

At 9:43 A.M., an American Airlines jet crashed into the Pentagon. It was Flight 77, out of Washington bound for Los Angeles. Like the two planes that crashed in New York,

⋆ ⋆ ⋆ ⋆

Flight 77 had been hijacked by a team of five terrorists. The hijackers gained control of the plane somewhere on the trip west and flew the plane back to Arlington, Virginia.

The terrorists zeroed in on the Pentagon. With fifty-eight passengers and six crew members on board, the plane flew at high speed into the west side of the Pentagon. The fuel on board the plane exploded, setting the building on fire.

The west side of the Pentagon was so badly damaged that part of the building collapsed. Army and navy offices were destroyed. One hundred and twenty-five people working in the Pentagon were killed, as were all sixty-four people on the plane. Working in his office in the Pentagon, Secretary of Defense Donald Rumsfeld felt

THE PENTAGON

The Pentagon is one of the world's largest office buildings. The U.S. Capitol could easily fit inside the five-sided building. It covers 29 acres (12 hectares) and is home to 23,000 employees. More than 17 miles (27 km) of hallways run through the building. It was opened in 1943.

Secretary of Defense Donald Rumsfeld, who was in the Pentagon at the time of the attack

15

the building shake. Looking out of his window, he could see smoke billowing from the Pentagon. As the fire burned, Rumsfeld hurried from his office to help lead injured workers to ambulances. The fires at the Pentagon burned for two days before firefighters were able to put them out.

THE CRASH OF FLIGHT 93

As the Pentagon burned, another plane headed toward Washington. United Flight 93 took off from Newark, New Jersey, and was headed to San Francisco. There were thirty-seven passengers and seven crew members on board. Somewhere over Ohio, four terrorists on board took control of the plane. They turned the plane to the southeast, so it was pointed straight at Washington.

The four hijackers carried knives. One of them had a box, which he claimed was a bomb, strapped to his body. As one of the terrorists flew the plane, passengers used their cellular phones to call loved ones. By now it was nearly ten o'clock in the morning. Some of the passengers learned about the earlier attacks on the World Trade Center and the Pentagon. They must have thought that the terrorists planned to crash their plane, too.

Some of the passengers on Flight 93 decided to fight back. A passenger named Tom Burnett called his wife on the phone. He told her that he knew the terrorists planned to crash the plane. But some of the passengers "are going to do something about it," he said.

* * * *

Jeremy Glick, another passenger, called his wife, too. "We're going to rush the hijackers," he said. "Our best chance is to fight these people rather than accept it." Others on board prepared for a struggle. A flight attendant in the plane's kitchen boiled water to use as a weapon. A telephone operator listening in on a phone conversation heard a passenger named Todd Beamer say to his fellow passengers, "Are you guys ready? Let's roll." There were screams. Then the phone went dead.

At 10 A.M., Flight 93 crashed in a field in western Pennsylvania. Everyone on board was killed. By fighting back, the passengers on Flight 93 may have prevented the terrorists from crashing the plane somewhere in Washington, D.C. They lost their lives but may have saved many others. Later, Vice President Richard B. Cheney paid tribute to the heroes of Flight 93: "Clearly, we know the plane was headed for Washington. Without question, the attack would have been much worse if it hadn't been for the courageous acts of those individuals on Flight 93."

THE PLANES

American Airlines Flight 11 was a Boeing 767 with eighty-one passengers and eleven crew members on board. The plane was headed from Boston, Massachusetts, to Los Angeles, California. American Airlines Flight 77 was a Boeing 757 with fifty-eight passengers and six crew members on board. It was headed from Washington, D.C., to Los Angeles, California.

United Airlines Flight 93 was a Boeing 757 with thirty-seven passengers and seven crew members on board. It was going from Newark, NJ, to San Francisco, California. United Airlines Flight 75 was a Boeing 767 with fifty-six passengers and nine crew members on board. It was headed from Boston, Massachusetts, to Los Angeles, California.

American soldiers stationed in Saudi Arabia during the Gulf War

The U.S.S. *Cole* returns to Mississippi after taking heavy damage from a bomb. A tarp covers the hole that was ripped in its side.

Mayor Rudolph Giuliani speaks about healing the city at a press conference on September 26, 2001.

THE TOWERS COLLAPSE

In New York City fires raged. High up in the twin towers of the World Trade Center, temperatures reached as high as 2,000 degrees Fahrenheit (1,093 degrees Celsius)—hot enough to melt steel. Amazingly, thousands of people were able to walk down stairs to escape the fires. Others were not able to reach safety. They jumped out of windows to escape the intense heat and fell to their deaths. Ambulances, police cars, and fire trucks arrived from all over New York to help with the emergency. Doctors and nurses rushed to nearby hospitals to treat the injured. Mayor Rudolph Giuliani walked the streets of the city, helping to maintain order during the emergency.

* * * *

New York City firefighters set up a command post at the base of the towers. Even as the towers burned, firefighters walked into the buildings to rescue people and put out fires. They walked up the stairs, floor after floor, carrying heavy equipment. As they walked up, office workers hurried down to escape. The office workers cheered the firefighters as they passed.

Firefighters were still going into the buildings when yet more tragedy struck. At 10:05 A.M., the south tower collapsed to the ground. A massive cloud of dust and smoke filled the streets of lower Manhattan. Where the 110-story building once stood, there was only a pile of twisted steel and broken concrete. Less than half an hour later, the north tower also crumpled to the ground. The twin towers of the World Trade Center had disappeared.

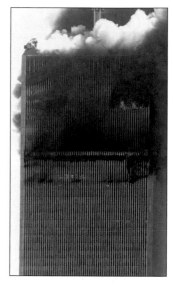

The north tower of the World Trade Center engulfed in smoke and fire

Sheik Omar Abdel Rahman, one of nine people convicted of taking part in the 1995 World Trade Center bombing

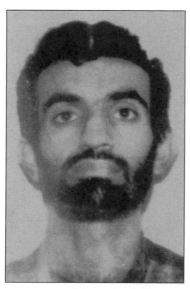

Ramzi Yousef, who was convicted of planning the 1995 World Trade Center bombing

THE FIRST WORLD TRADE CENTER BOMBING

The attacks of September 11 were not the first on the World Trade Center. In 1993 bombs planted in a truck parked beneath the towers killed six people and injured hundreds. In 1995 Sheik Omar Abdel Rahman and nine others were convicted of taking part in the attack. In 1998 Ramzi Yousef was convicted of planning the bombing. Yousef, Rahman, and the others shared the same extreme beliefs as Osama bin Laden and his al Qaeda followers.

★ ★ ★ ★

An ambulance races toward the burning World Trade Center towers.

Why did the tall towers come crashing down? They were held up by 244 steel **girders**, or support beams. Each of these girders was designed to support the weight of the floors above. However, the steel girders were weakened by the intense heat of the burning jet fuel. Steel starts to bend at 1,000 degrees Fahrenheit (537° C). Some of the girders became so weak that they could no longer support the building's weight. Once they gave way, other girders had to hold more weight. They too gave out under the heavy load. Very quickly the top floors of the tower began collapsing onto the floors below. In a chain reaction that took just seconds, the towers collapsed. Hundreds of rescue workers had no chance to escape the crush of the falling buildings. Nearly four hundred firefighters died in the disaster.

Firefighters search for survivors after the collapse of the twin towers.

OSAMA BIN LADEN AND AL QAEDA

Osama bin Laden was born in Saudi Arabia around 1957. He was one of more than fifty children born to a businessman and his several wives. His father, who came from Yemen, became a billionaire building roads and structures in Saudi Arabia. Bin Laden inherited part of his father's fortune. In the 1980s bin Laden fought in the war between Afghanistan and the Soviet Union. He was one of many Muslims from other countries who helped Afghans defeat the Soviet invasion of their country.

In the 1990s bin Laden moved back to Saudi Arabia. He was out-raged when the Saudi government allowed American troops to be stationed in Saudi Arabia during the Gulf War (1991). Saudi Arabia is home to some of the most sacred places in Islamic culture. Bin Laden believed that the presence of Americans there was an insult to Islam.

In the 1990s bin Laden began building a terrorist organization to attack American targets. The group was called al Qaeda. In 1998 the group exploded bombs outside American embassies in Nairobi, Kenya, and Dar es Salaam, Tanzania. The bombs killed 224 people and injured about four thousand others. In 2000 al Qaeda struck again. Bombs exploded near the American warship U.S.S. Cole, stationed in Yemen. The explosion killed seventeen American sailors.

Osama bin Laden, as seen in video footage on October 7, 2001

A Soviet tank leaves Afghanistan and crosses the border back to the USSR.

Damage to the U.S. embassy in Dar es Salaam, Tanzania after a car bomb exploded outside it

THE INVESTIGATION BEGINS

Almost immediately, federal authorities began investigating who was responsible for the attacks. The Federal Bureau of Investigation (FBI) assigned four thousand special agents and three thousand other staff to the case. These agents fanned out across the country to track down leads. Local police departments assisted in the case, as did investigators from around the world. Government officials later learned that the hijackers were members of a terrorist group called al Qaeda (Arabic for "the base"). Al Qaeda was founded by a wealthy Islamic man, a native of Saudi Arabia named Osama bin Laden. (Islam is one of the world's great religions, with more than one billion believers worldwide. Followers of Islam are called Muslims. Extreme Muslims, like bin Laden and his followers, make up a small part of the world's Muslim community.) Bin Laden and his followers are committed to attacking the United States. They consider the Western way of life evil and resent America's power and influence around the world. They believe the U.S. oppresses, or treats harshly and unfairly, Muslims all over the world.

Smoke and rubble were all that remained of the twin towers by the evening of September 11, 2001.

23

The Qu'ran is the holy book of Islam, from which Muslims learn the teachings of their religion.

Al Qaeda members come from many countries. They gather at top-secret camps to learn the **tactics** of terrorism, and to prepare for terror assignments years in advance. Al Qaeda sends these students of terror to live in the United States, Europe, and elsewhere, where they form so-called sleeper cells. A sleeper cell is a loosely organized group of terrorists waiting for instructions to commit an act of terror. While they wait to strike, they may work at jobs or attend school so that they appear to be like any ordinary member of a community. Indeed, some of the hijackers who struck on September 11 had been living in the United States for years, waiting for their orders to attack. Some went to school in the United States to learn to fly. They planned the attacks carefully. They armed themselves with small homemade knives that airport security guards did not notice. They split up into teams of four or five terrorists for each hijacked flight. They probably chose to attack on a Tuesday because fewer people fly on Tuesday than on any other day of the week. This meant there would be fewer people on each plane for the hijackers to control. They chose only flights whose destination was California because these long-distance flights would be fully loaded with explosive fuel that could turn them into deadly weapons.

The Empire State Building towers above the rest of the skyline in New York City.

A NATION UNDER SIEGE

Following the collapse of the twin towers people throughout the United States prepared for more attacks. No one knew where terrorists would strike next. New York City officials stopped traffic from coming into the city on bridges and tunnels. They evacuated the Empire State Building, once again the tallest building in New York. The **headquarters** of the United Nations closed. New York's airports shut down.

Later in the morning, all other airports across the country closed. Airplanes stayed on the ground and all five thousand planes

★ ★ ★ ★

United Nations headquarters, which closed down soon after the attack

in the air were brought down safely. It was the first time in history that commercial air traffic in the United States completely stopped.

In Washington, **sharpshooters** took up positions on the roof of the White House. Secret Service agents hurried into the office of Vice President Dick Cheney, and led him away to a safe place. Senator Robert Byrd, Speaker of the House Dennis Hastert, and other congressional leaders were also taken to safe locations.

As a safety precaution, America's most famous **landmarks**, such as Disney World, Mount Rushmore, and Independence Hall in Philadelphia, were all closed. So was the Sears Tower in Chicago, America's tallest building.

Vice President Cheney (left), Senator Robert Byrd (center), and Speaker of the House Dennis Hastert (right) were all taken to safe locations following the attacks.

Mount Rushmore (above) and Independence Hall (left) closed for safety reasons following the attacks.

★ ★ ★ ★

The Sears Tower in Chicago, Illinois, was shut down after the attacks. As America's tallest building, it was feared that it would be a prime target if there were further attacks.

★   ★   ★   ★

ABOARD AIR FORCE ONE

The Secret Service feared that terrorists might attack President Bush. After learning of the attacks in New York, the president planned to return to the White House from Florida. However, people wondered if even the White House was safe. Instead, Air Force One and the president headed for Barksdale Air Force Base in Louisiana. While on Air Force One, the president talked on the phone with Vice President Cheney and his top advisers and cabinet members. Bush touched down at the air force base just long enough to deliver a message to the nation on television. "Freedom itself was attacked this

AIR FORCE ONE

Air Force One is the call sign, or radio code name, for any air force plane that carries the President. As soon as the president steps on board any U.S. Air Force plane, that plane becomes Air Force One. The president usually flies on one of two identical planes that are set aside for vhis use. The planes are Boeing 747s, the world's largest aircraft. They stand as high as a five-story building. Inside are offices for the president and his staff, sleeping quarters for the president and his family, and two kitchens that can prepare one hundred meals. It's no wonder that Air Force One is sometimes called the "flying White House." Air Force One also comes with top secret security features, including high-tech weapons systems that can fight off missile attacks.

Air Force One takes off from Barksdale Air Force Base in Louisiana.

29

Offutt Air Force Base in Omaha, Nebraska played a critical role in allowing President Bush to keep in touch with officials throughout the country.

morning by a faceless coward," Bush said. "Make no mistake, the United States will hunt down and punish those responsible for these cowardly acts."

Then the president got back on board Air Force One and headed for Offutt Air Force Base in Nebraska. Offutt Air Force base is the home of U.S. Strategic Command Headquarters, a high-security, high-technology command center for the military. Inside its huge rooms are video screens that stand several stories tall and computer terminals that can track military activities around the world. There he continued to work, staying in touch with officials in Washington and all over the country. At 3:30 P.M., the president conducted a video meeting of the National Security Council, a group of **cabinet** officers and other department heads responsible for the national defense. George Tenet, the director of the Central Intelligence Agency, briefed the president on al Qaeda's connections to the hijackings. Vice President Cheney, Secretary of Defense Runsfeld, and FBI Director Robert Mueller also participated in the meeting. The president announced his determination to return to Washington to address the people once more, this time from the White House. His Secret Service protectors still advised against returning to Washington, but Bush overruled them.

Finally, the President returned to the White House just before 7 P.M. About an hour and a half later, he delivered a speech on national television. The president told Americans, "our fellow citizens, our way of life, our very freedom came under attack in a series of deadly and **deliberate** terrorist acts. The **victims** were in airplanes or in their offices: secretaries, business men and women, military and federal workers, moms and dads, friends and neighbors." He promised to find and punish the people who committed "these evil acts." The president continued, saying, "These acts were intended to frighten our nation. . . . But they have failed. Our country is strong."

Bush also sent a strong and clear signal to other international leaders that he expected their cooperation in the war against terrorism. "We will make no distinction between the terrorists who committed these acts and those who harbor them," Bush said. With that statement he made it clear that any nation that gave aid or shelter to terrorists would be subject to U.S. military action.

At dusk the following day leaders of Congress gathered on the steps of the Capitol. The group included members of both the Democratic and Republican parties. Speaker of the House of Representatives Dennis Hastert spoke for all of them. "When Americans suffer and when people perpetrate acts against this country, we as a Congress and as a government stand united and stand together," Hastert

Members of Congress sing "God Bless America" during a prayer vigil on the steps of the Capitol on September 12, 2001.

said. He asked everyone to bow his or her head in silence. Then the senators and members of Congress sang "God Bless America."

THE WORLD REACTS

World leaders were shocked and angered by the attacks. Russian president Vladimir Putin called the attacks "terrible tragedies" and sent good wishes to the American people. Prime Minister Tony Blair of Great Britain pledged to support the United States in its war on terror. "This mass terrorism is the new evil in our world today," Blair said. "And we the democracies of the world are going to have to come together and fight it together." Sweden's prime minister Goran Persson agreed that "all democratic forces must form a united front."

Palestinian leader Yasser Arafat said he was shocked by the attacks and told the American people he was sorry for their losses. However, many Palestinians cheered the attacks. About three thousand gathered on the streets of the town of Nablus to celebrate just after the attacks. The United States government is unpopular with many Palestinians, who believe the United States does not support their effort to create a Palestinian nation.

AFTER THE ATTACKS

In the days after the attacks, Americans vowed to remember the victims and to fight terrorism. On September 12, first lady Laura Bush went to a Washington hospital to visit victims of the attack on the Pentagon. The next day, she

First lady Laura Bush, who assured schoolchildren that they would be safe

wrote a letter to schoolchildren assuring them that the United States is "looking out for your safety." Congress approved spending $40 billion to combat terrorism and rebuild areas damaged by the attacks.

President Bush declared September 14 a national day of prayer. At a prayer service at the National Cathedral in Washington, he paid tribute to people who lost their lives and to people who tried to save others. He told Americans that it was the nation's responsibility to "rid the world of evil." At other prayer services all over the country and all over the world, people joined the president in remembering the victims.

A prayer service was held in the National Cathedral in Washington, D.C., on September 14, 2001.

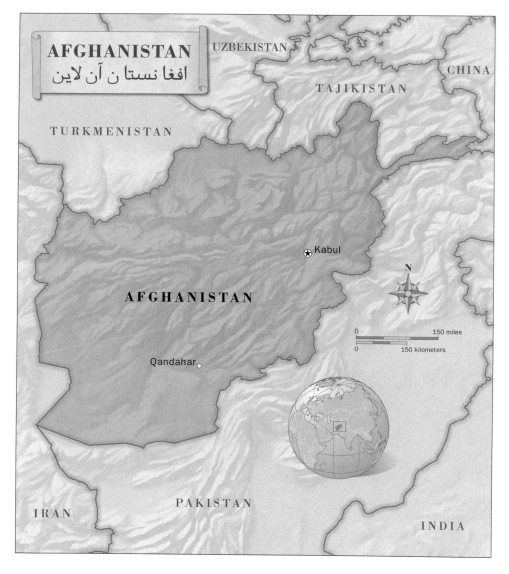

AFGHANISTAN

افغا نستا ن آن لاین

UZBEKISTAN

CHINA

TAJIKISTAN

TURKMENISTAN

★ Kabul

AFGHANISTAN

Qandahar

0   150 miles

0   150 kilometers

IRAN

PAKISTAN

INDIA

The United States attacked Afghanistan in hopes of destroying the headquarters and main support of the al Qaeda terrorist network.

At the same time, the United States prepared to strike back at Osama bin Laden's al Qaeda terrorist group. Al Qaeda was based in Afghanistan, where it received support from the government. In October, U.S. planes began attacking targets in Afghanistan. Their goal was to drive the Afghan government from power and to destroy al Qaeda

TERRORISM'OS HISTORY

Terrorism is the threat, or use, of unexpected violence against civilians or their government leaders to achieve political goals. Terrorists carry out assassinations, bombings, hijackings, and other crimes to scare people and governments into meeting their demands. Terrorism is not new. The ancient Greek historian Xenophon (431–350 B.C.) wrote about armies that tried to break the spirit of their enemies by attacking civilians. In the twelfth century, Middle Eastern terrorists murdered their enemies to gain power. They were called the Assassins. Eventually, anyone who killed for political gain was called an **assassin**. In the late 1800s terrorists killed kings, presidents, and prime ministers in Europe and the United States, attempting to bring about political change.

A statue of Xenophon, the ancient Greek historian who wrote about terrorism

terrorist bases in Afghanistan. Al Qaeda worked closely with the government of Afghanistan, a group called the Taliban. The Taliban shared many of Osama bin Laden's extreme religious beliefs. They deprived women and ethnic minorities of basic human rights. U.S. and British forces and Afghan rebels teamed up to win a quick victory, driving the Taliban from power. However, they failed to catch Osama bin Laden. At the start of 2002 the hunt for bin Laden went on.

Meanwhile, the terrorist attacks did not end. In late 2001 five people died after touching mail that had been intentionally contaminated by anthrax. Anthrax is an infectious disease usually found in farm animals. By the end of 2001, U.S. investigators still did not know who was responsible for the anthrax mailings or if they were directly related to al Qaeda.

In December a terrorist on a flight from Paris to Miami tried to set off explosives that he had hidden in his shoe. He was stopped by other passengers and flight attendants. If he

People wore protective clothing when handling any mail they suspected had anthrax on it.

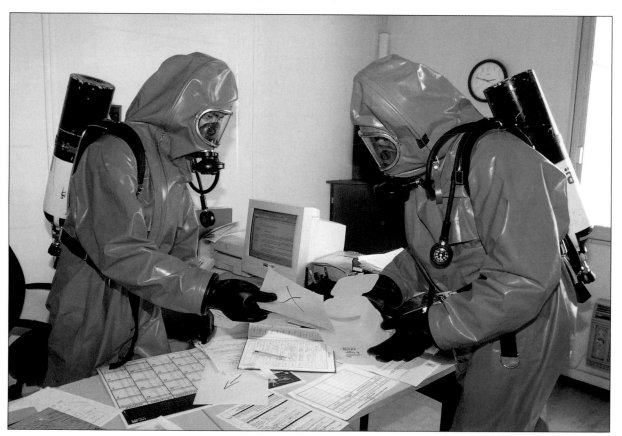

had succeeded in setting off the explosives, the blast might have killed more than 197 people on board. Investigators later learned that the passenger, Richard Reid, had trained with the al Qaeda **network** and may have known some of the September 11 hijackers.

REMEMBERING SEPTEMBER 11

The attacks of September 11 were unexpected and devastating. Most Americans had come to believe that their country was safe from foreign attack. September 11 proved them wrong. The terrorist attacks took the lives of military men and women, rescue workers, and ordinary citizens. In all, about three thousand people are believed to have died. The attacks toppled two of America's greatest landmarks, the towers of the World Trade Center. They damaged the Pentagon, a symbol of U.S. military might. Many of these horrible events were recorded live on television as millions of Americans watched.

On March 11, 2002, people around the world stopped to remember the heroes of September 11. Exactly six months had passed since the attack on America. At the White House, President Bush spoke to three hundred relatives of victims of the attacks. Also in attendance were members of Congress, leaders of the U.S. military, and members of the president's cabinet. The president remembered September 11 as a day when the world "was stirred to anger and to action." He pledged that the United States would continue to lead the fight against terrorism around the world. "I will not relent on this struggle for the freedom and security of my country and the civilized world," the president said.

At the Pentagon on March 11, Defense Secretary Rumsfeld led another memorial service. On hand were representatives of twenty-nine countries working with the United States to combat terrorism. Rumsfeld said that the attacks were "truly an attack against the world. Citizens from more than eighty countries died that day, men and women of every race and every religion. So the United States was not alone." Rumsfeld visited the spot where American Airlines flight 77 crashed into the Pentagon.

In New York City, officials dedicated a monument to the victims of the attacks on the World Trade Center. They unveiled a sculpture called "The Sphere" that had once stood outside the World Trade Center. The sculpture was created in 1971 by artist Fritz Koenig as a monument to world peace through trade. The sculpture was damaged during the attacks, but later it was recovered and repaired. Now it once again stands as an emblem of peace. New York governor George Pataki said the sculpture would "serve as the symbol of our never forgetting those heroes who died on September 11th, and our never forgetting that good will overcome evil."

People gather around "The Sphere," which honors the victlms of the World Trade Center attacks.

39

★ ★ ★ ★

That night in New York, twelve-year old Valerie Webb switched on eighty-eight searchlights. The lights were arranged to create two tall towers of light that climbed into the air where the World Trade Center once stood. Valerie's father, Port Authority Police Office Nathaniel Webb, was one of the people missing as a result of the attack.

"The lights will reach up to the skies and into heaven, near where the heroes are now," said Arthur Leahy, the brother of New York Police Officer James Leahy, who died on September 11.

In Shanksville, Pennsylvania, church bells rang in memory of the forty-four people killed there on September 11. Hundreds of people visited the site of the crash, in a field near town. They laid flowers next to a bronze monument that reads: "This memorial is in memory of the brave men and women who gave their lives to save so many others. Their courage and love of our country will be a source of strength and comfort to our great nation."

Not surprisingly, the attacks alarmed and frightened a lot of Americans. In spite of that, many Americans responded with acts of bravery, generosity, and patriotism. The passengers of Flight 93, the rescue workers of New York, and the military men and women of the Pentagon all became heroes. People across the country donated blood to victims of the attacks. All over the United States, people flew flags from homes, offices, and even their cars.

The horrible events of September 11 made the United States determined to fight terrorism. The government and airlines worked to tighten security at airports. Police in

The two towers of light representing the twin towers were a temporary memorial. The lights were switched on every night for thirty-two consecutive nights in memory of the lives lost in the attacks of September 11.

American cities kept watch on suspected terrorists. People rallied behind American troops fighting in Afghanistan. "We are a country awakened to danger and called to defend freedom. . . ." President Bush announced. "Freedom and fear are at war." The United States launched its war on terror to make sure that Americans would never know another day as tragic as September 11, 2001.

Glossary

assassin—a person who murders for political
    or religious reasons

cabinet—the group of government department heads and
    other advisers assembled by the president to help
    him lead the government

deliberate—intentional; done with full understanding
    of what one is doing

ethnic—belonging to a group of people who speak
    a common language

explosive—capable of blowing up

girders—heavy beams that hold up a building
    or other structure

headquarters—the base or main center of a company
    or military unit

hijacked—took control of an airplane by force

ignited—started a fire or caused an explosion

landmarks—buildings or features of the land that
    are easily recognizable

network—a collection of connected people or groups
    working for a common purpose

onlookers—people who stop and gather to watch
    an event or accident as it happens

sharpshooters—people who shoot guns with
    great accuracy

tactics—the plans or strategies used to accomplish
    something

victims—the people who suffer from an injury, accident,
    or other destructive action

Timeline: September 11,

September 11, 2001

8:45 A.M.
American Airlines Flight 11 flies into the north tower of the World Trade Center in New York City.

9:03 A.M.
United Airlines Flight 175 crashes into the south tower of the World Trade Center.

9:40 A.M.
The Federal Aviation Administration stops all airplane takeoffs in the United States.

9:43 A.M.
American Airlines Flight 77 crashes into the Pentagon.

9:57 A.M.
President George W. Bush speaks to the nation on television from Florida. He says the United States has suffered "an apparent terrorist attack."

10:00 A.M.
United Airlines Flight 93 crashes about 80 miles southeast of Pittsburgh, Pennsylvania.

10–11:30 A.M.
Major American landmarks such as Disney World and the St. Louis Arch are closed down.

2001

10:05 A.M.
The south tower of the World Trade Center collapses.

10:10 A.M.
A portion of the Pentagon collapses.

10:29 A.M.
The north tower of the World Trade Center collapses.

1:04 P.M.
President Bush, speaking from Barksdale Air Force Base in Louisiana, pledges that those responsible for the attacks will be brought to justice.

1:48 P.M.
President Bush leaves Barksdale Air Force Base and flies aboard Air Force One to Offutt Air Force Base in Nebraska.

4:30 P.M.
President Bush leaves Offutt Air Force Base aboard Air Force One, bound for Washington.

6:54 P.M.
President Bush returns to the White House.

8:31 P.M.
President Bush speaks to the nation and promises to punish "those responsible for these evil acts."

To Find Out More

BOOKS

Marsh, Carole. *The Day That Was Different: September 11, 2001: When Terrorists Attacked America.* Peachtree City, GA: Gallopade Publishing, 2001.

Santella, Andrew. *Air Force One.* Brookfield, CT: Millbrook Press, forthcoming.

Sherrow, Victoria. *The World Trade Center Bombing: Terror in the Towers.* Berkeley Heights, NJ: Enslow, 1998.

ONLINE SITES

A Sad Day in History
http://wire.ap.org/APpackages/attacks_kids_flash/

September 11, 2001: A Turning Point in History
http://turnerlearning.com/fyi/turningpoint/index.html

Time Magazine For Kids
www.timeforkids.com

Index

Bold numbers indicate illustrations.

About the Author

Andrew Santella writes for magazines and newspapers, including *Gentlemen's Quarterly* and the *New York Times Book Review*. He is the author of several Children's Press books, including *The Battle of the Alamo* and *Mount Rushmore*.